PASSING

MW00957163

Passing
THE
TORCH

CRITICAL CONVERSATIONS
WITH YOUR ADULT CHILDREN

BOB MAUTERSTOCK

16 15 14 13   10 9 8 7 6 5 4 3 2 1

Passing the Torch
ISBN-13: 978-1505395204

Copyright © 2014 by Bob Mauterstock

Printed in the United States of America. All rights reserved under International Copyright Law. Contents and/or cover may not be reproduced in whole or in part in any form without the express written consent of the Publisher.

DEDICATION

This book is dedicated to my beautiful wife, Mary. Throughout my career she has been the source of my success. She has always been my guiding light, focusing me on what is important and freeing me up to do what I do best.

"The essence of communication is intention"

Werner Erhard, 1973

ACKNOWLEDGEMENTS

I would like to acknowledge my daughter, Stephanie, for inspiring me to take on this project. Without her insistence that I provide her with financial advice I never would have realized the value of guiding her and other young people on the path to financial literacy.

I'd also like to thank my editor, Lauren Helper, for her consistent, timely and superior editing skills. This is our second project together and I hope there will be many more.

I want to thank Nancy Fleming and Deb Fish for introducing me to the mediation process and training me to become an effective facilitator. They are truly brilliant guides.

I'd like to thank the many clients I've had over the years who have taught me the value of communication between generations. Those who weren't successful taught me just as much as those who were.

I want to thank Werner Erhard for creating the EST Training which transformed my relationship with my parents, my wife and my daughter.

CONTENTS

1

INTRODUCTION

After I wrote my first book in 2008, *Can We Talk? A Financial Guide for Baby Boomers Assisting Their Elderly Parents*, I spoke to a number of people in their 50s and 60s about the importance of opening up communication with their elderly parents. I got a lot of feedback and questions from individuals about their own personal situations.

One of the comments I often heard was, "Your book has helped me a great deal in getting my parents' situation in order, but now I've realized I need to talk to my own children, so they know my circumstances and wishes. I don't know where to start and what to do."

I looked at my own life and realized I had made the same mistake. I had conversations with my mother and father and helped them get their lives in order, but was scared to death about sharing my own plans with my daughter. Every time I brought up the topic of end-of-life planning, I would start and my daughter would say, "Dad, let's not talk about that now. You are doing fine." And I would immediately change the subject and breathe a sigh of relief.

But one day I was preparing for a presentation to a group of financial planners in Florida. I was reviewing my lines that stressed the importance of sharing your plans with your family, when I suddenly realized that we had never gotten around to having that conversation in our family. Fortunately my daughter was going to be with us the weekend before I traveled to Florida.

I came up with a plan that I thought would work. I shared with her the presentation I was going to make, and when I came to the section discussing end-of-life planning, I slipped in my own plans. My daughter didn't flinch and surprisingly asked a number of intelligent questions. I now felt I could approach my audience with honesty. I had taken the leap myself.

After I had faced reality and made the effort to clean up my own communication, I decided to write this book to help others. My decision was reinforced by a study I read produced by Merrill Lynch in partnership with Ken Dychtwald and the Age Wave Organization.

The study is titled "Family & Retirement: The Elephant in the Room," which originated from a survey completed by 5,415 respondents, including 2,104 Boomers (aged 47-67). The study reached a number of very interesting conclusions, some of which were shocking, but frankly, not surprising.

The study determined that the two greatest retirement worries facing Baby Boomers were:

1. Living a long life and running out of money.

2. Becoming a burden on the family.

They defined "being a burden" primarily as the need for family members to "physically take care of" them.

How many of us have discussed with our children our plans for care as we get older? Have we shared with them our thoughts on the following?:

1. Where we intend to live if one of us needs extended care.

2. Who we expect to take care of us.

3. How we will pay for this care.

In this book I will discuss each of these issues, including how to formulate answers and share them with our children.

Another very important finding of the study related to proactive communication between Boomer parents and their children. It stated, "Most people are reactive, not proactive when discussing important financial decisions with family members."

It added, "Active Discussions and coordination with family members can be the difference between smooth sailing and significant hardship when confronting family challenges throughout retirement."

The study found that 70% of adult children 25 and older have not had an in-depth discussion with their parents about their parents' retirement issues. Only one in four (24%) have discussed with their parents what their expected financial situation will be during retirement and who will care for them if they need extended care.

This book is designed to prepare you to have those important conversations with your adult children. It will give you the tools you need to plan your retirement years with them. Reports show that retirees who have in-depth conversations about the critical issues of retirement are twice as likely to be well-prepared to face the family challenges of aging.

The book is divided into two sections. The first section, I call the "Lifefolio." It is structured to help you get your financial life in order. This is important to complete before you meet with your children. If you are not certain of your resources and your plans, it will become blatantly obvious when your children start to ask you questions about your future.

The Lifefolio will require you to gather up your financial statements, wills, trusts and other important documents. Once you have done this, you will immediately feel a sense of relief, knowing that if an emergency should occur, all the necessary information will be easy to get your hands on. I have learned how valuable this is after watching many families go through the agony of trying to locate important information and documents after a family member is stricken.

I'll also ask you in the Lifefolio to take a stab at defining your legacy, spelling out what has been important to you in your life and what you want to pass on to the next generation. You may never have thought about this before, but your children will thank you for it once you have put it together.

The second section of the book is "Giving the Gift of Communication." Here is where you prepare for, plan out and begin your conversations with your children. This is where the rubber hits the road. I will ask you to determine what your money attitude is, and what you have shared with your children about money in the past. We will take a look at how to improve your listening skills so you can really "be" with your family.

I will give you specific advice on how to prepare for and hold a family meeting. There are eight important steps to follow to make this meeting successful. I am confident in saying that if you follow these steps, your family meeting will be a life-altering experience. You will begin to communicate with your children on a whole new level. I have witnessed this experience myself and have been deeply moved to watch it unfold.

Finally in the last chapter of the book, I will ask you, "What's Next?" This chapter is designed to help you plan out your future interactions with your children and help them formulate their own financial plans. It's a guide for positioning yourself as their mentor and guide for their future life experience.

I am excited to share this book with you. I challenge you, as a parent, to take on this responsibility, to share your hopes, your dreams and accomplishments with your children, to take them on as partners in living out the rest of your life. At some point in the process you may hesitate and become uncomfortable, but if you press on, the results will be well worth it. You may find this to be one of the most fulfilling experiences of your life.

2

THE LIFEFOLIO

I describe the gathering together of all the quantitative information in your life as the "Lifefolio." It's a place where you keep
all the account numbers, documents and dollar values that define
your financial life.

It is important to establish one central location to maintain
all your financial records. During my 33-year career as a financial advisor, I observed many clients who were facing a family
emergency and couldn't find the important documents and information they needed to get things done to handle their affairs.
Don't let this happen to you. If you are like many of us, your
information is scattered in several different places, some of which
your family doesn't even know exists. Let's get that corrected!

You have several options for collecting and maintaining your
financial information. The method you choose should be the one
you are most comfortable with. Some people like the tangible
quality of a traditional notebook. Others are more comfortable
with an internet-based system. The most important thing is that
you select a system that works for you and regularly maintain it.
Here are several options that I recommend.

Three-Ring Binder

The simplest way to manage your records is to use a dedicated three-ring binder to list important information and the location of important documents. **I have created a 36-page document that will help you gather all the important information you need.** This PDF document is a result of working with clients for over 30 years and learning what was important to them. You can print out the forms or use them as an online PDF, entering the data online and then printing it out. You can save it on your computer or on a thumb drive.

Send me an email at Bob@giftofcommunication.com and I will email the form to you.

Once you complete the forms and establish the binder (or have saved online), make your family aware of its location. Select a binder with a colorful cover so you can't lose it! And keep the binder updated. If anything changes, change it in the binder or change the PDF online. Otherwise your binder will become outdated and worthless.

Digital Solutions

If you are more comfortable keeping your Lifefolio online or on a computer, you can utilize a number of other solutions.

Computer-based

The two most popular computer-based financial recordkeeping systems that I am aware of are Quicken (available for Mac and PC) quicken.intuit.com and IBank 5 (available for Mac) www.iggsoftware.com. These systems allow you to keep track of investments and bank accounts. They integrate directly with your bank and investment companies, allowing you to download transactions as they occur. You can even use them to pay bills and keep track of your budget.

However, they are not particularly adept at keeping track of insurance policies and legal documents. The advantage of these computer-based systems is their ability to automatically update your investment values and your banking records. To maintain records of your insurance, legal documents and other non-financial data, you would need to supplement the systems with spreadsheets or Word documents that hold this information. Therefore I don't consider them particularly attractive choices as your primary recordkeeping system.

Internet/Cloud-Based

If you have a financial advisor, you may have access to an excellent money management tool that is internet-based. It is known as the emoney advisor (www.emoneyadvisor.com). I have used a version of it available to advisors that are affiliated with LPL Financial. It is known as Wealthvision. It is the most sophisticated internet-based financial planning system that I am aware of. You can keep track of all investments and bank accounts daily, no matter where they are located. You can list all insurance products (life, health, disability, long-term care, etc.) that you own with details of each policy. You can store copies of your legal documents and you can do all kinds of financial projections using your actual data (retirement, education funding, savings plans, etc.). Once you have this system you will never want to lose it.

If you don't have a financial advisor or you want to create your own internet-based recordkeeping system, you can utilize a cloud-based system such as Dropbox or Google Drive.

The downloadable Dropbox desktop application runs on Windows, Mac or Linux operating systems and gives you access to your Dropbox directly through a folder on your hard drive.

In addition to using the Dropbox website, you can download and install the Dropbox desktop application to get the most out of the system. Using Dropbox on your computer is just like using any other folder on your hard drive, except the files you drag into your Dropbox folder automatically sync online and to any other computers or mobile devices linked to your account.

The desktop application *even works when you go offline.* The next time you're online, Dropbox will sync changes just where it left off.

You can scan important legal documents or insurance policies and upload the files to Dropbox. You can save the forms you filled out with your financial information on Dropbox. You can also designate people you are willing to share any of these files with like your spouse, professional advisor or children.

Google Drive is very similar to Dropbox. Essentially, it's a beefed-up version of Google Docs. You can store your documents, photos, music, videos, etc. all in one place. It syncs with your mobile devices and your computer, so if you make a change from one gadget, it will automatically show up if you access it elsewhere.

It tracks your changes too, so if you make an edit to the document and hit save, you can still look back at all your revisions from the past 30 days. Of course it relies heavily on Google search, with image recognition for browsing your photos and some OCR capabilities for sniffing out text in pictures. It easily integrates with all of Google's other applications such as Gmail, Google Images and the social marketing tool Google+.

The Information Gathering Process

Once you have chosen the medium you want to use to store all your financial information, it is now time to gather it all together in one place. Let's go through the material you need to save.

1. *Insurance and Annuity Policies*

When you were issued any type of life, disability, long- term care insurance policy or annuity, you received a document specifying the coverage provided and the policy's legal limitations. You need to locate all of these policies. Once you find them you need to write down the name of the insured, the policy number, the insurance company, the type of policy and the amount of coverage that you have for each. Record all of this on one sheet. For life insurance policies and annuities, you also need to determine who the beneficiary is (the person who will receive the benefits when the insured dies).

If by any chance the beneficiary is no longer appropriate (an ex-spouse, a deceased parent), you can write the company and request a change of beneficiary form. Beneficiary forms should also be saved with the policy. If you discover that a policy is no longer in force, it is important to destroy it so your heirs will not be confused and try to receive the benefits from a cancelled policy.

Once you have recorded all this information, decide where you will keep the policies and note that on the form. A fireproof metal box that is easily accessible is a good place to store them.

2. *Investments and Bank Accounts*

If you are like most of us, you probably have investments and bank accounts in a number of places. First, identify the banks or investment companies that hold your accounts. Then list the account number for each. Investment accounts and bank accounts can be owned in different ways, including joint ownership with a spouse, sole ownership or ownership by a trust. Specify the ownership and the approximate current value of the account.

Finally, if you can access the account through the internet, record the website address, username and password to access the account. It is very important to keep this information up to date. If you are sick or unable to access your accounts, no one else can access them without this information. I will discuss this further in a section on digital estate planning.

3. Legal Documents

If you have done any form of estate planning with an attorney, you probably have a number of legal documents. We will discuss which documents you must have and the purpose of these documents in more detail in another section. Legal documents include wills, trusts, durable powers of attorney and health care proxies. Determine if you have copies of any of these documents. If you can't find them at home, you might want to check to see if they are stored at your attorney's office. Identify the name of the document, when it was signed and where you intend to keep it on a one-page form. Again, an easily accessible fireproof box is a good place to retain it.

4. Key Advisors

Over the years you have probably established relationships with key advisors. If something happened to you, your family might need to contact these people. They can include a banker, insurance agent, financial planner, attorney, primary care doctor, specialty doctor, accountant and religious leader. You might also have close friends or associates who are very familiar with your affairs. List the names of these people, their relationship with you, and their street address, email address and phone number.

5. Retirement Accounts

As part of your retirement planning, you most likely will have some sort of retirement vehicle. These can include an IRA,

Pension Plan, Social Security, 401(k) plan, or profit sharing plan. List the company or organization the plan is through, the current value or monthly income expected and if it provides for payment to a beneficiary. If there is a provision for a beneficiary, you need to identify who that beneficiary is. If that beneficiary is no longer appropriate, you should contact the organization to find out how to change it.

6. Liabilities

If you have a mortgage or any other form of debt, it is important to list these. Mortgage debt should include the institution holding the mortgage, the amount of the outstanding mortgage, the mortgage number, the interest rate and monthly payment. Credit card debt should list the card company, the card number, approximate balance and contact information.

7. Digital Estate Planning

In the past we kept albums full of snapshots, vinyl records and shoeboxes full of correspondence. Now our photos are all on Flickr or IPhoto, our music is downloaded from ITunes and our correspondence is emailed via Yahoo or Google. Recently I created a spreadsheet of all my important internet accounts and I listed more than 25. Your situation is probably similar.

You need to create a listing of all your digital assets. This spreadsheet should include:

- The name of the account

- The contents of the account

- The URL Address

- Your username

- Your password

- Instructions for the disposition of the account including the person to oversee such disposition.

It is important to keep this spreadsheet up to date. If you don't, the listing will become worthless.

Once you have gathered together all this information, recorded it in your lifefolio and placed any documents in a safe, accessible place, you can congratulate yourself for your work. Believe it or not, you have done more planning and organization than 90% of your friends and associates! You should feel a sense of pride and accomplishment for getting all this information together.

Now that you have completed this arduous, time consuming but extremely valuable task, we can begin the review of your financial plans, the next step in preparing for the critical conversations with your family.

3

LEGAL ISSUES

There are a few documents that you should have in place to avoid legal problems for yourself or your children. Let's take a look at each one to determine its importance to you.

Wills

First and most important is the will. This document states what will happen to your property when you die. If you do not complete a will, you will die "intestate." That means the state in which you reside will decide what happens to your assets. The court will name an executor, who will oversee the closing of the estate and charge a healthy fee to do so. In each state, the rules may be different as to who gets what. But one thing is certain—the process will take longer than desired. It will cost more money and your wishes won't be carried out exactly the way you intended.

If you have never drafted a will, you might resist doing so the first time. Creating a document that states what happens when you die may feel ominous. To set it up, you have to admit that you are actually going to die. One of my clients went through the entire process of planning his estate with an attorney. He and his wife met with the attorney several times and hammered out all the details of who was going to get what. But a few months later, I got a call from the attorney. He said, "Bob, I still haven't heard back from your client. His unsigned will is sitting on my desk." I called my client and he made some excuse about not having the time to stop by the attorney's office. He finally signed the will right before he and his wife were flying to Hawaii on vacation. I guess he finally admitted that he could die in a plane crash.

You and your spouse should each have your own will. The will doesn't have to describe what happens to each object that you own, but should lay out your general wishes. "I leave my tangible property to . . ." etc. You can attach a Letter of Instruction to the will to identify specific items that you want to go to individuals. This Letter of Instruction can be changed from time to time without having to redraft the will. You can complete it yourself and add it to the will.

I suggest strongly that you use an attorney to help you draft the will. **You want to be absolutely certain that the will is an official legal document in the state that you reside. A local attorney will make sure of that.** I'm sure you have heard of a number of software programs out there that provide the basics of will writing. But you can't be sure that your state would recognize that particular format as legally binding. Don't take the chance. Select an attorney who is familiar with estate planning. Ask your friends and associates if they know a good estate-planning attorney. You don't want to use someone who primarily deals with real estate closings and only one or two wills per year.

In many cases you may decide to designate your spouse to receive all your assets and then if he or she is deceased, the assets will be divided equally among your children. But are you absolutely certain that you want to have the assets divided equally? What happens if you have one child who is a single mother living hand to mouth and another child who has done very well financially? Does it make sense to divide things equally between them or do you want to pass on more of your assets to the child who is having difficulties? This may be an important topic for a family meeting, which I will discuss later.

You may also choose not to divide your assets equally if you want to recognize one or more children for working hard and becoming successful. I have heard of situations where a client divided his assets among his children based on the income they showed on their tax return. More income was rewarded with a greater share. Or you may choose some other criteria to reward your children. Once again it is important that you communicate these decisions to your children while you are alive. It might create a real breakdown in their relationship with each other if they are unaware of your plans until your will is revealed after your death.

I had a client who was one of three sons working in their father's waste management business. When the father died, he named one son to take over the business in his will, leaving the other two as employees. This had never been discussed before his death. The two disenfranchised sons left the business and started a competitor. They never spoke to their brother again.

You may have noticed that you have designated a person to be the executor or executrix (female) in your will. This position is also called the "Personal Representative". The executor's responsibility is to carry out your wishes as stated in the will and keep track of any financial transactions that ensue. The job requires attention to detail. Make sure that you have selected the right person (and they are still available). It's often a good idea to name someone younger than yourself to be more certain that they will be around when you pass.

Trusts

There are other cases where you might want to make special provisions for your children based on their unique circumstances. In these cases you may want to use a trust to fulfill your wishes.

First, let's define what a trust is. A trust is a legal entity that separates the legal ownership of property from the beneficial ownership of property. In a trust, one person or a group of persons (the trustees) hold assets (the corpus) for the benefit of one or more other people (the beneficiaries). The person who creates the trust by transferring his or her money, property, or assets to the trustee is the grantor or settlor of the trust. The terms and conditions of the trust are specified in the Trust Document. It is the trustee's job to make sure that the provisions of the trust are carried out in accordance with the wishes of the grantor as stated in the trust document. The trustee has a very important role, described as a fiduciary responsibility, to make sure the terms of the trust are followed.

There are essentially two types of trusts: living trusts and testamentary trusts. The Living Trust is an intervivos trust, which means it is set up during the grantor's lifetime and it is effective while you are alive. A Testamentary Trust is created by your will and does not take effect until you die.

Let's take a look at a few examples of trusts that might be helpful to you to make sure your wishes are carried out. If you have a child who has had an accident or has some physical impairments and as a result has a physical or mental disability that qualifies them for government aid, a "special needs trust" may be appropriate.

Your attorney needs to understand the specific needs of your child with the disability and be familiar with local, state, and federal programs upon which your child may depend for lifetime care and support. A special needs trust provides that the trustees distribute funds from the trust for items not provided by the government. Under current law, a properly worded special needs trust is not considered a countable asset of the beneficiary and will not prohibit them from getting government aid.

I had a client whose son had been in a motorcycle accident and had suffered severe brain damage. He was living in a group home but was unable to earn enough money to support himself. He qualified for government assistance but was also able to receive income from a "special needs trust" that his father had set up.

You may have a child whom you just don't trust managing money. He or she might just be a spendthrift or might have a more serious problem involving drugs or alcohol. You can set up a trust for them with all distributions of income or principal controlled by an individual or corporate trustee.

You can also use a trust to protect funds for your grandchildren if you don't trust your child's spouse. Depending on your situation, a good estate planning attorney can design the trust that is right for you.

The trustee named in your trust is the person who is responsible to carry out the provisions of the trust. You may have named yourself, another person, a bank or an institution to be a trustee. You can combine any of the above to be trustees. Be sure to follow your attorney's recommendations in naming trustees. Also determine under what circumstances the trustee can be relieved of their duties. If it is yourself or another individual, make sure you allow for replacement if the trustee is no longer mentally or physically competent. It is also possible to name successor trustees in this case.

Durable Powers of Attorney

In addition to a will, the durable power of attorney is a document you must have. Without a durable power of attorney, your spouse or your children cannot act on your behalf in financial matters if you are incapacitated. One of my clients became very ill. He was in the hospital when I called his home to suggest that he transfer an investment from one fund that was performing poorly to a CD with a higher interest rate. He needed to sign a document to make the transfer. If his wife had a durable power of attorney, she could have signed the document for him. She didn't have the authority, so we had to wait until he was well enough to do it himself.

You may use this document many times. It allows the "attorney in fact" to act on your behalf, sign checks for you, sign legal documents, etc. It should be updated every two to three years. Selecting someone to have the durable power of attorney is an important decision. You should give your spouse this power and another person, a family advisor or one of your children whom you consider responsible and trustworthy.

I don't suggest that you give the power of attorney to more than one child. This dilutes the responsibility and culpability of the job. Name one child and name another as a successor or backup.

The Beneficiary Statement

If you own any life insurance policies, annuities, IRAs, or other retirement plans, these investments all pass to the named beneficiary on the beneficiary statement. When you set up these accounts, you filled out a beneficiary statement. This beneficiary statement asks you to name primary and contingent beneficiaries. The primary beneficiary is usually your spouse and the contingent is usually your children, divided in some percentage amount amongst them.

It does not matter how you have your wills set up. The funds will automatically pass to the named beneficiary on the beneficiary statement. For example, even though your will says that everything should go to your wife, if your life insurance beneficiary statement indicates that the life insurance proceeds go to your brother, then your brother will get that money.

Review your beneficiary statements. Make sure the beneficiaries listed are correct. If you cannot find the beneficiary statement or wish to change the beneficiary, contact the appropriate institution. They will send you a new form to make changes or replace a lost form.

It is important to name both primary and contingent beneficiaries. If your primary beneficiary is deceased, the proceeds will go to the named contingent beneficiaries. If no contingent, the assets will be included in your estate and possibly trigger additional taxes and fees.

As I stated in the first chapter, record all this information in your Lifefolio. Remember that your will does not have any impact on your IRAs, life insurance policies, annuities, and other retirement plans. Only the beneficiary statement for each will decide who will get these assets.

Now that we have discussed your basic legal requirements, in the next chapter we will focus on what you would do if you or your spouse suffer a long- term illness. We will look at the options available to you and how to prepare yourself for that possibility.

4

CREATING A LONG-
TERM CARE PLAN

Have you ever discussed with your spouse or your children what would happen if one of you suffered a long-term chronic illness? Would you stay in your home? Who would take care of you? How would you pay for your care? Unfortunately, most families don't deal with these questions until a crisis actually occurs. Then, decisions are often made in a pressured environment without a great deal of thought or planning.

You may not realize it, but one of the greatest risks to your retirement security is the possibility of you or your spouse suffering a long-term chronic illness. Modern medical science has done wonders to reduce the loss of life due to cancer, heart disease and other ailments. But as a result, you or your spouse (or possibly both of you) may need some form of care for a long period of time at some point in the future.

According to a study done by the National Institute of Health, an estimated 37 million Americans were age 65 or older in 2006. That was 12 percent of the population. In 2030, it is estimated that 71.5 million people or 20 percent of the population will live to be over 65.

The U.S. Department of Health and Human Services reports that 70 percent of these people turning age 65 can expect to need some form of long-term care during their lives.

We all hope to live a long, healthy life and won't need extended care, but doesn't it make sense to make plans now for the possibility that you or your spouse will need help? A recent study by Merrill Lynch concluded that Baby Boomers' two greatest fears during retirement are:

1. Running out of money before they run out of time

2. Becoming a burden on their family

By "becoming a burden on their family" the respondents meant "having family members physically take care of them." Boomers don't want their children to eventually be forced to become their caregivers.

So what do you do to avoid forcing your children to become your caregivers at some point in the future? Develop a plan now! But where do you start in creating this plan?

1. Understand what resources are available to you to pay for care

Medicare

If you get sick and spend at least three nights in a hospital, your physician can refer you to a rehab center to recover. As your care is focused on rehabilitation or skilled care, Medicare will cover the expenses incurred if you are 65 or older. You will pay nothing for the first 20 days and a $152 copay for days 21-100. The average Medicare-covered stay is twenty-two days.

Medicare-covered services include, but aren't limited to:

- Semi-private room (a room you share with other patients)

- Meals

- Skilled nursing care

- Physical and occupational therapy

- Speech-language pathology services

- Medical Social Services

- Medications

- Medical supplies and equipment used in the facility

- Ambulance transportation (when other transportation endangers health) to the nearest supplier of needed services that aren't available at the SNF (skilled nursing facility)

- Dietary counseling

Currently, Medicare provides limited coverage for expenses incurred for rehabilitation if you choose to go home.

Medicare covers up to thirty-five hours per week of skilled nursing care and home health aide services. You may also receive additional hours of skilled physical and occupational therapy and other social services. The amount of covered services allowed in the plan of care depends on your doctor's recommendation.

Realistically, based on what Medicare pays home health care agencies, you can expect to receive about ten hours of care per week at home. Services and supplies approved in the plan of care are covered in full. Durable medical equipment is covered at 80 percent of the Medicare-approved amount. **But please note: Medicare will not cover chronic or custodial care if you are not expected to recover.** Your doctor or the rehabilitation facility generally makes that determination.

Medicaid

Many people are confused about the differences between Medicare and Medicaid. Medicare only provides payment for a person who is recovering from an illness or injury. It does not provide ongoing custodial care. Medicaid is a program jointly funded by the federal and state governments to provide assistance to the indigent who need custodial care. A third of the payments from Medicaid provide payments for the elderly who are in nursing homes. Other funds are provided for those who are disabled or without financial resources. Medicaid does not currently provide any benefits for assisted living or in-home care; it is strictly for those individuals who are in a nursing home.

To qualify for Medicaid, you must meet strict income and asset limitations. In 2014 the income limit ranges from $1,938 to $2,422 per month. Monthly income limits differ depending on whether the applicant is single or married. For a married couple, the spouse remaining in the community (known as the "community spouse") can retain all of his or her income. The community spouse's income would not be counted in determining the applicant's eligibility for Medicaid. However, all of the applicant's income must be counted for his or her long-term care except for certain deductions.

To qualify for Medicaid coverage, the recipient's countable assets cannot exceed $2,000. Countable assets consist of all investments such as stocks, bonds, mutual funds, checking and savings accounts and CDs. Countable assets also include any personal or real property as well as any art and collectibles.

The amount of resources that the healthy spouse (the community spouse) is allowed to keep is called the community spouse resource allowance (CSRA), and it varies by state. Medicaid sets a minimum and maximum CSRA that the state CSRA may fall within, but the states are allowed to choose from a wide range. In 2014, the federal maximum CSRA is $117,240, and the federal minimum is $23,448. These limits can change every year. Check with your state's Medicaid agency to find out how much in resources you are allowed to keep in your state.

Based on these requirements, it is very unlikely that you will qualify for Medicaid unless your income is very low and you have depleted all your assets in paying for care. If you are approaching that point, I strongly suggest that you contact an attorney who is a specialist in elder law and is a member of the National Academy of Elder Law Attorneys (NAELA, www.naela.org). These attorneys can help you deal with the very complicated restrictions and requirements of Medicaid.

Veterans Long-Term Care Benefits

The Department of Veterans Affairs provides three types of long-term care benefits for veterans.

The first type of benefit is provided to veterans enrolled in VA health care who have a substantial service-connected disability. These medically-necessary services include home care, hospice, respite care, assisted living, domiciliary care, geriatric assessments and nursing home care.

Some of these services may be offered to veterans in the health care system who do not have service-connected disabilities but who may qualify because of low income or because they are receiving pension income from the VA. These recipients may have to provide out-of-pocket co-pays or the services may only be available to these non-service-connected disabled veterans if the regional hospital has funds to cover them.

Currently, veterans desiring to join the health care system may be refused application because their income is too high or they do not qualify under other enrollment criteria. Increased demand in recent years for services and lack of congressional funding have forced the VA to allow only certain classes of veterans to join the health care system.

The second type of benefit is provided by state veterans homes. The US Department of Veterans Affairs, in conjunction with the states, helps build and support state veterans homes. Money is provided by the VA to help share the cost of construction with the state, and a daily subsidy is provided for each veteran using nursing home care in a state home. These facilities are generally available for any veteran, and sometimes for spouses of veterans, and are run by the states, often with the help of contract management. Most state veterans homes offer nursing home care but they may also offer assisted living, domiciliary care and adult day care. There may be waiting lists for acceptance into veterans homes in some states.

State veterans homes are not free, but are subsidized. However, the cost could be significantly less than a comparable facility in the private sector. Some of these homes can accept Medicaid payments. A complete list of state veterans homes can be found at http://www.longtermcarelink.net/ref_state_veterans_va_nursing_homes.htm.

The third type of benefit for veterans is the disability payment. These include compensation, pension and survivors' death benefits associated with compensation and pension.

Compensation is designed to award the veteran a certain amount of monthly income to compensate for potential loss of income in the private sector due to a disability, injury or illness incurred while in military service. In order to receive compensation, a veteran has to have evidence of a service-connected disability. Most veterans who are receiving this benefit were awarded an amount based on a percentage of disability when they left the service.

However, some veterans may have a military record of being exposed to extreme cold, an in-service, non-disabling injury, a tropical disease, tuberculosis or other incidents or exposures that, at the time of exposure, may not have caused any disability, but resulted in medical problems years later. In addition, some veterans may already be receiving compensation, but their condition has worsened and they may qualify for a higher disability rating and thus a higher compensation. Veterans mentioned above may qualify for a first-time benefit or receive an increase in compensation amount. Applications should be submitted to see if they can receive an award. There is no income or asset test for compensation and the benefit is nontaxable.

Pension is available to all active duty veterans who served on active duty at least ninety days including one day beginning or ending during a period of war. There is no need to have a service-connected disability to receive pension. To be eligible, the applicant must be totally disabled if he or she is younger than 65. Proof of disability is not required for applicants age 65 or over. Apparently, being over age 65 is evidence in itself of disability. Pension is sometimes known as the "aid and attendance benefit."

Pension can pay up to $1,758 a month for a veteran, $1,130 per month for a surviving spouse, $2,085 a month to a married vet and $2,788 to two married veterans. This amount changes each year and is tied into the cost of living. It is received tax-free. The funds are provided to help offset the costs associated with home care, assisted living, nursing homes and other unreimbursed medical expenses. The amount of payment varies with the type of care, recipient income and the marital status of the recipient. There are income and asset tests to qualify.

Eligibility must be proven by filing the proper Veterans Application for Pension or Compensation (Form 21-534 for surviving spouses, Form 21-526 for veterans).

Long-Term Care Insurance

What do you do if Medicare runs out at the end of your rehabilitation period and you don't qualify for Medicaid or veteran's benefits? You can use up your investment and retirement assets to pay for care or you can tap into your home equity using a reverse mortgage or a home equity loan. But if you plan ahead and apply while both you and your spouse are healthy, you can utilize long-term care insurance.

During my thirty-three years as a financial advisor, I've seen many families whose retirement assets were protected because they had purchased long-term care insurance. One of my clients was working part time as a newspaper reporter at the age of seventy-one. Her husband was a retired executive. Based on my recommendation, they had both purchased long-term care while they were in their sixties.

Unfortunately, the husband was diagnosed with Parkinson's disease. His wife was able to care for him while he was still in the early stages of the disease; but bad luck struck their family twice. She suffered a stroke and was no longer able to take care of herself, much less her husband. Their long-term care insurance covered the cost of aides to take care of both of them at home. Every time I met with them after that, they thanked me for recommending the insurance.

In the past, many advisers and financial authorities were very cynical about long-term care insurance, but that has changed dramatically in the last ten years. Long-term care insurance has improved significantly in this period of time. Companies have improved benefits and expanded coverage to provide at-home care, adult day care and assisted living facilities, as well as nursing homes.

In addition, the Internal Revenue Service (IRS) has provided additional tax incentives for individuals who own long-term care insurance. If any individual receives a long-term care benefit from an insurance company, it may be considered tax-free income. Check with your tax advisor for details. Policyholders can also deduct a portion of their premiums as a medical expense based on their age. Each year the IRS publishes a table to determine the amount of a premium that you can deduct.

The IRS has also made it attractive for businesses to provide long-term care insurance coverage to their key people. In the traditional corporation, a business owner can select key people (including himself or herself) and have the business pay for the long-term care for those employees and their spouses without it being considered taxable income to that person. In addition, the business can deduct what it spends on the premium. Finally, if any employee or spouse receives benefits from the policy, the money received is not taxable. The government has made long-term care a benefit with significant tax advantages for the employer and employee.

To qualify for payments under most long-term care policies, a doctor must certify that the person is unable to do two or more of the activities of daily living. These activities include bathing, toileting, eating, transferring in and out of bed, dressing and walking. Cognitive impairment from dementia or Alzheimer's disease is also covered.

The biggest objection to buying coverage comes from those people who think long-term care insurance is too expensive, but the cost of care is much more expensive. In the Northeast, where I live, the cost of a stay in an assisted living residence is between $5,000-8,000 per month. Nursing homes costs can exceed $10,000 a month. These monthly payments can deplete your investments very quickly. Paying $5,000 a year for long-term care insurance is far less expensive than paying $10,000 per month for care.

If you are unwilling to pay the costs of long-term care insurance, there are other options. The industry has developed several hybrid products that provide long-term care insurance as well as other permanent benefits. One of these is a life insurance policy that incorporates long-term care insurance within it. This type of policy can be purchased with a one-time payment or, in some cases, an annual premium like traditional life insurance.

One of my clients told me he was not interested in paying long-term care premiums that he would never recover if he didn't need the care. He purchased a life insurance policy with a single payment of $100,000. He immediately had $165,000 of life insurance if he died. At the same time, he was able to choose a long-term care benefit equal to two percent of the death benefit for four years as part of the policy. This meant that his life insurance policy would pay up to $3,300 per month for long-term care for four years. If he did not use the long-term care benefit, the life insurance benefit would be paid out to his beneficiary at his death. If he did use the long-term care benefit, the life insurance death benefit would be reduced to a minimum guaranteed amount. In this way, he felt he was getting the full value for his premium dollars.

In addition to life insurance policies, some annuities have long-term care benefits. These annuities accumulate at a guaranteed rate of interest and build up a cash fund that can be used to pay for long-term care. As long as the interest is deferred in the annuity, you do not pay taxes on the gain. The gain is only taxed (as ordinary income) when you make withdrawals from the contract. If the cash value of the annuity is not used to pay for long-term care, you can pass on the annuity to your heirs. Unlike life insurance, however, the beneficiary must pay taxes on the gain when they receive it. Life insurance benefits are received tax-free.

2. Where do you want to live if you need care?

Staying in Your Home

In a recent AARP study, nearly 75% of adults 45 and older said they strongly desire to stay in their current home as long as possible. To make sure that you can "age in place," you may have to make several updates to your home and your financial plan. Do not expect that your children or the government will step in and help you out. You need to create a plan to take care of yourself.

In addition to concerns about transportation and the availability and cost of help, you need to take a serious look at your home. Don't wait until there is a crisis to make needed improvements. Are your doorways wide enough to accommodate a wheelchair? A narrow wheelchair or walker needs clearance of at least thirty-two inches.

Is your master bedroom on the first floor? If not, are the steps to the second floor steep and is the stairway narrow? You may have to consider some sort of stairway elevator to get up and down at some point. Do you have a full bathroom on the first floor? If so, does it have a walk-in shower? Converting a bathtub to a walk-in shower may cost somewhere between $3,000-5,000. This is likely one of your most costly changes.

Look at your faucets and cabinet handles. Are they big enough to access with a closed fist? Check out your lighting. Older eyes need more light to see clearly. Check to see that the lighting is good in areas where tasks are performed. Consider the interior colors in your home. If your home has dark floors, keep the walls light. Change the color at potential tripping points, such as where the carpet meets a hard-surface floor area. Are there other step-ups or step-downs in the home where it is possible to trip and fall?

You need to review access to the home itself. In addition to the entry way being wide enough for a wheelchair or walker, is there room to install a ramp for access if necessary?

Do not wait until someone is coming home from the hospital to consider these steps. Look around now and start planning to make the changes that will help you stay in your home. Most of the suggestions listed above will not only make your home safe and accessible, but they will probably increase its market value as well.

Alternatives to Home Care

There are certainly other options to staying in the family home. As 10,000 Baby Boomers reach retirement age each day, most who need care will not plan to enter an assisted living residence and will never step foot into a traditional nursing home. Increasing numbers will seek out new alternatives for independent living where care can be provided.

Intentional communities for philosophical, religious and lifestyle groups are emerging. Wikipedia describes an intentional community as, "A planned residential community designed from the start to have a high degree of social cohesion and teamwork. The members of an intentional community typically hold a common social, political, religious, or spiritual vision and often follow an alternative lifestyle. They typically share responsibilities and resources."

Alex Mawhinney (jamlll@charter.net), a developer of retirement communities for over twenty-five years, reports that, **"Intentional elder neighborhoods are becoming the new paradigm for elder living."** He states that Boomers will no longer be interested in "The older generation of elder living options that our parents used," which follows this model:

1. Age in place, in a home not designed for aging in place, and eventually live alone

2. Move in with children or other relatives

3. Move in to an institution and pay dearly for care delivered by strangers, under their rules and according to their schedules; the institution might be a nursing home, an assisted living facility, a rest home, a retirement hotel, or a continuing care retirement community with multiple levels of care

These elder neighborhoods are taking many different forms. It would behoove you to determine if any of them have been created in your community.

A national movement of local "villages" to provide care and help elders stay at home is growing. There are now more than 125 of these villages throughout the country. In my community, the "Nauset Neighbors" program offers more than 150 volunteers who provide services to elders for a very reasonable annual fee. These services include transportation, maintenance and support services, technical support for cell phones and computers and friendly visits. The member has to make only one call to Nauset Neighbors and a voluntary call manager will coordinate the service. Read more about them at www.nausetneighbors.org.

There are also SOTELs (service-oriented, technically-enhanced living, like an upscale Embassy Suites), ecovillages, senior cohousing and the new lifestyle communities like those being developed by Canyon Ranch.

The common traits of these new alternatives are that they are:

- Human-scaled (not large and impersonal)

- Relationship-based

- Resident-managed/centered, with an overlay of lifelong learning and later-life spirituality

- Focus on giving back to the community

3. Who Will Care For You?

Have you ever discussed who will care for you or your spouse if one of you needs long-term care? Will you care for each other or do you expect another family member to be your primary caregiver?

If you, as the healthy spouse, choose to become the primary caregiver for your sick partner, it can put a very heavy burden on you. **As a result of caregiving for a long period of time, the healthy spouse may become a second sick spouse.** Generally caregivers provide care for their spouse for an average of four to five years. Twenty-two percent of these spousal caregivers suffer from depression.

One of my clients had a stroke at age seventy. He is a very big man who was an active golfer, but he lost all the strength and movement in his right side. His wife chose to take care of him at home. She was not able to get him in and out of bed by herself, so she hired an aide to come in the morning and to return again at night. For the rest of the day she acted as his caregiver. As a result, for the last five years, she has been homebound and unable to take any trips or visit any friends. She limits her time away from the home to one or two hours per day to do grocery shopping or run errands.

More than 65 million people, 29 percent of the U.S. population, provide care for chronically-ill, disabled or aged family members or friends and spend an average of 20 hours per week providing care for their loved one.

The typical family caregiver is a 49-year-old woman caring for her widowed 69-year-old mother who does not live with her. The caregiver is likely married and employed. Approximately 66 percent of family caregivers are women. More than 37 percent have children or grandchildren under 18 years old living with them.

If you ask one of your children or the spouse of one of your children to become a caregiver for you, it puts an added burden on the family. It is even more difficult if both parents are not well and there is no family member nearby to act as the caregiver. In these cases, if you want to stay in the home, a professional aide must be hired.

The cost to have a health care worker in your home is approximately $20-25 an hour in most areas of the country. You may be able to find someone less expensive if you are very lucky, but you would have to hire them directly and not through an agency. The advantage of using an agency is that they have done background checks on their workers and they usually have the resources to provide you with another person if the first one doesn't work out. Also, they handle all the details of payroll and insurance. If you hire someone directly, you take responsibility for his or her character and all the rules required for insurance and payment to an independent contractor.

It is very important for you to discuss with your spouse and children the difficulties of becoming a caregiver if you choose to stay in your home. Each of you must be fully aware of the challenges and responsibilities of such a role before you take it on.

4. Consult Your Financial Advisor

The possibility that you or your spouse may need extended care should be an important part of your retirement plan. If you have a financial advisor, make sure that he or she prepares projections showing you the impact of long-term care on your retirement finances. Compare the cost of financing the care from your own resources versus the use of long-term care insurance. These projections will help you create a realistic plan that you can share with your family.

Once you have created a long-term care plan for yourself and your spouse, it is time to address one of the most difficult and uncomfortable challenges that you will face: End of Life Planning. This is an area that most of us want to avoid as long as possible. But my experience has shown me that families that plan for their inevitable demise while they are healthy will create a result that is far better for the entire family than if they had not planned at all.

5

END OF LIFE PLANNING

Planning for the last days of your life is probably the most difficult planning you will ever need to do. Certainly no one wants to contemplate their death, but experience has shown that those people who plan ahead will save their families much grief and anxiety.

Ellen Goodman, a journalist for the *Boston Globe*, is the co-founder of an organization called "The Conversation Project." After her mother's death, she discussed with a number of her media colleagues, clergy and medical professionals the experience they had when their own parents died. She learned that they could classify their experiences into "good deaths" and "bad deaths."

She discovered that those families who had taken the time to discuss their parents' hopes and fears regarding their end-of-life plans had a much more positive family experience than those who had ignored the subject.

Ellen had a very difficult time when her mother died. She said, "We talked about everything except one thing; how she wanted to live at the end of her life." And she added, "The last thing my mom would have wanted was to force me into such bewildering, painful uncertainty about her life and death. I realized only after her death how much easier it would have all been if I heard her voice in my ear as these decisions had to be made."

As a result of her experience, Ellen created the Conversation Project (www.theconversationproject.org). This non-profit organization is dedicated to helping people have the conversation with their family regarding their end of life plans. Their website can provide you with a "starter kit," offering you guidelines to help you prepare for and have the conversation with your loved ones.

Ellen suggests that there are four steps you should take in the process. The first is "Get Ready." It is a time to think about the end of life and perhaps write a letter to yourself, a loved one or a friend.

The second step is "Get Set," to figure out what you want your end-of-life care to be. What kind of care do you want to receive? How involved do you want your loved ones to be? Who do you want to make the decisions?

The third step is "Go," deciding who you need to talk to and when a good time would be to have the conversation. I strongly recommend that you begin with your spouse or partner and share your wishes with your children at a Family Meeting. I will discuss this more in the next section of the book.

The fourth step is "Keep Going," preparing the legal and medical documents that you need to back up your wishes. These documents include the following:

The Health Care Proxy: This is a legal document that identifies who will make the difficult health care decisions if you are unable to make them. This person is often called the health care agent and the document is often called the Durable Power of Attorney for Health Care. It is very important that you select a person who understands what your wishes are and is willing to carry them out. It may be your spouse, one of your adult children, a friend or an advisor. It is also important to name a successor for this role if the agent is unavailable.

The Living Will: This is also known as an advance health care directive. It is a set of instructions that you give to specify what actions should be taken for your healthcare if you are no longer able to make those decisions for yourself. By itself it is not a legal document, but it gives direction to your health care proxy regarding your wishes for end-of-life care.

The best document that I have seen that combines the Health Care Proxy and the Living Will is "The Five Wishes" available from www.agingwithdignity.org. It guides you through the process of determining your end-of-life wishes and determining whom you want to represent you. It is often described as "a living will with soul." The Five Wishes include:

- The Person I Want to Make Decisions for Me When I Can't
- The Kind of Medical Treatment I Want or Don't Want
- How Comfortable I Want to Be
- How I Want People to Treat Me
- What I Want My Loved Ones to Know

With the signatures of two witnesses, this document is legal in forty-two states. The website lists which states are included. I would strongly suggest that you complete this document, share it with your spouse, your primary care doctor and your estate attorney. In addition you should share it with your children at The Family Meeting described in the next section.

HIPAA Form The Health Insurance Portability and Accountability Act of 1996 ("HIPAA") was established to assure that individuals' health information is properly protected. In order to get any information regarding a family member who is hospitalized, you must show this form (signed by the patient) to the hospital staff.

Without the HIPAA release form, the hospital will not give your family members any information about your current health condition. Therefore it is important to provide your family with a signed HIPAA form before you go into the hospital. A printable HIPAA Release form is available at: http://www.mobar.org/uploadedFiles/Home/Publications/Legal_Resources/Durable_Power_of_Attorney/final-hipaa-fillable.pdf

Do Not Resuscitate (DNR) Form Although you may have completed a living will and prepared an advance directive identifying a health care proxy, you have not yet covered all the bases for end of life care.

Advance Directives and living wills are not accepted by Emergency Medical Services (EMS) as legally valid forms. If you have a living will stating that you do not wish to be resuscitated but you do not have an appropriately filled out state sponsored Do Not Resuscitate (DNR) form that is co-signed by a physician, the Emergency Medical Technician (EMT) will attempt resuscitation in an emergency. This is a little known fact to many patients and primary care physicians that can cause patients to be resuscitated even if their family has given instructions not to do so. Although this law is currently being evaluated for a constitutional challenge, it is still in place.

A DNR document is a binding legal document that states resuscitation should not be attempted if a person suffers cardiac or respiratory arrest. A DNR does not affect any treatment other than that which would require intubation or CPR. Patients who are DNR can continue to get chemotherapy, antibiotics, dialysis or any other appropriate treatment. Most likely you would not sign a DNR form unless your illness was terminal and you did not wish to be resuscitated if your heart failed.

The DNR documentation is especially complicated since each state has its own specific approved form. The DNR form for residents of the State of Arizona is required to be printed on orange paper or it is not valid. The Massachusetts form can be obtained from the Department of Emergency Services and can be downloaded from the site: http://www.mass.gov/eohhs/docs/dph/emergency-services/comfort-care-form.pdf.

It is imperative that you contact your state health and human services department to determine what form is approved in your state. The form must be signed by the health care proxy and cosigned by a physician. It is recommended that the original DNR form be kept in safe place, and that copies be kept in places that will be readily available to EMS personnel. A hospice nurse informed me that the first place EMT's will look for a DNR form is the door of the refrigerator. Make sure you post it there for your family member if they are at home.

The POLST Form

POLST stands for Physician Orders for Life Sustaining Treatment. It is a new form, available in a few states, that gives seriously ill patients more control over their end-of-life care, including medical treatment, extraordinary measures (such as a ventilator or feeding tube) and CPR.

The POLST Paradigm is an approach to end-of-life planning emphasizing: (i) advance care planning conversations between patients, health care professionals and loved ones; (ii) shared decision-making between a patient and his/her health care professional about the care the patient would like to receive at the end of his/her life; and (iii) ensuring patient wishes are honored.

As a result of these conversations, patient wishes may be documented in a POLST form, which translates the shared decisions into actionable medical orders. The POLST form assures patients that health care professionals will provide only the treatments that patients themselves wish to receive, and decreases the frequency of medical errors.

The National POLST Paradigm originated in Oregon in 1991 as leading medical ethicists discovered that patient preferences for end-of-life care were not consistently honored. Recognizing that advance directives were inadequate for the patients with serious illness or frailty—who frequently require emergency medical care—a group of stakeholders developed a new tool for honoring patients' wishes for end-of-life treatment.

Although the POLST Paradigm began in Oregon, it quickly spread to other states, which tailored the paradigm to fit their unique legal, medical and cultural contexts. Among the first states to develop POLST Programs were New York, Pennsylvania, Washington, West Virginia and Wisconsin. These states—and others—have become leaders in improving the POLST Paradigm and demonstrating its importance to achieving patient-centered outcomes.

You can go to the POLST site to determine if there is a POLST program approved in your state http://www.polst.org/programs-in-your-state/

Once you have planned out your end-of-life care and created the appropriate documents to support your wishes, you need to communicate your wishes to your family. We will discuss how to do this in Chapter 10, The Family Meeting.

6

LEAVING A LEGACY

During the last six months of my father's life, I visited him every week in his rehab facility. He was desperately trying to get well enough to return home. Because of his Parkinson's disease he could no longer swallow and therefore couldn't eat normally. But he could talk. And we would talk for hours every time I visited.

Most of our conversations were about insignificant things like sports teams, my job or the weather. We very rarely got into a real conversation. On one occasion I asked him what it was like growing up as the son of a minister. He told me that he had never gone to a department store to buy clothes. All his new clothes came from the barrel, where members of the congregation would toss clothes they didn't want.

He shared that in the first eighteen years of his life, he had moved eleven times as my grandfather was transferred from church to church. But we never talked about his childhood again. And I never asked him about his experience as an Army engineer, landing at Omaha Beach on D-Day.

Six months after my father passed away, my mother asked me a question. "Did you ever look at Dad's scrapbook?" And she handed me a leather bound scrapbook filled with pictures, maps, newspaper stories, insignia and a letter signed by General Dwight D. Eisenhower. I was shocked. I had never known that this scrapbook existed.

For the last fifteen years I have leafed through that scrapbook hundreds of times, wishing that I had the opportunity to learn from him what his experience was like. But I will never get the chance. I share this with you because I want to emphasize the importance of sharing your stories and experiences with your children.

How did you and your spouse meet? What was it like growing up? What were your parents like? Where did you go to school? What was it like? Our children want to hear about these things. And we need to share them.

There are several ways to share your experiences and your life with your family. One is through the Family Meeting, which I will discuss in the next section. Another is to create an audio or video recording for them. The third is to write your personal biography. There is a national organization that can help you with this project. It is the Association of Personal Historians (www.personalhistorians.org). Through them you can find a professional in your area to help you. They will create a professional audio recording, video recording or book of your life with your input.

The Legacy Letter

But let's assume you are not ready to go to those lengths yet to record your life. The best way to start is to write a Legacy Letter. It is as simple as answering a series of questions in a letter format.

In her very informative book *The Wealth of Your Life, A Step-By-Step Guide for Creating Your Ethical Will*, Susan Turnbull suggests that creating the Legacy Letter is a five-step process. Here are her suggested steps:

1. Identify to whom you want to send the letter. Do you want to send an intimate letter to just family or a more public document to be read by many people?

2. Consider your intentions and opening lines. Start the letter with the brief statement of why you want to write it. "I am hoping to share many more wonderful years with you, but I wanted to make sure that you know . . ."

3. Reflect and make notes. What is your theme? Is it an opportunity to express your love to those close to you? Do you want to share the values that have been important to you that you want to be remembered for? Do you want to pass on the wisdom that your experience has taught you? Do you want to pass on the family history to the next generation? Jot down your thoughts. You may choose to include some or all of these themes in your letter.

4. Create an outline to structure the order in which you wish to make your points. Keep in mind your audience, your goals and the most important things you want to say.

5. Create your letter (or record it). I strongly suggest that you create a video of your words as well as a written document. In the video your words will come to life if you share them with enthusiasm and conviction. In this era of smartphones and sophisticated technology it will be very simple to create a video record. You can even post it on Youtube or Facebook if you so desire.

Helping a Charity

In addition to writing a Legacy Letter, you may want to be remembered by your college, your religious group or another organization that has been important to you. There are a number of ways to do this that not only benefit the organization, but benefit you as well.

The simplest thing to do is to name the organization in your will. This is known as a bequest. You can state that a specific amount of money or a percentage of your estate goes to the organization. It can be made as a restricted gift for a specific purpose, such as buying a new organ or benefiting the church school, or it can be an unrestricted gift allowing the organization to use the funds for whatever purpose they find necessary.

Another very simple way to make a contribution to a nonprofit organization is through life insurance. If you own a life insurance policy, you can change the beneficiary to name the charity as one of the beneficiaries. For example, if you have a $100,000 life insurance policy that you no longer need, you can split the primary beneficiaries between your family and a charity. All you need to do is submit a change of beneficiary form to the insurance company. You can specify the amount going to the organization or a percentage of the death benefit.

There are also other methods that you can use to benefit from the gift while you are alive. One of these is called a Charitable Remainder Trust (CRT). This is an arrangement in which property or money is donated to the charity, but the donor continues to receive income from it while they are alive. By donating property such as stock or real estate that appreciates significantly in value, you can avoid paying capital gains tax on the gift.

One type of Charitable Remainder Trust is called a Charitable Remainder Unitrust (CRUT). The CRUT is designed to pay an annual income to one or more persons (the beneficiaries) for a set period or for their lifetime. When the individuals give property or cash to a charity, the amount of income they receive is based on the value of the assets in the trust multiplied by a percentage rate that is determined when the trust is created. When they set up the trust, the person who makes the donation receives a current tax deduction that is calculated based on a number of factors.

There are other variations of the Charitable Remainder Trust. One is called the Charitable Remainder Annuity Trust (CRAT). Like the CRUT, the individual makes a gift of property, stock, cash, or some other form of capital to a charity. The charity then sells the property, invests the proceeds, and pays an income to the beneficiaries based on the terms of the trust. With the CRAT, the income amount stays the same each year no matter how much the principal changes. The CRUT income can vary because it is based on a specific percentage of the capital remaining in the trust each year.

One of my clients worked for a large corporation most of his life. He bought some of the company stock every year he worked there. By the time he was in his sixties, he had accumulated a large amount of the company stock. If he sold it, he would have had to pay a large capital gain. About that time, he was preparing to celebrate his 50th college reunion. As a gift to the college, he placed a large portion of the stock in a charitable remainder trust that the college offered. As a result, he was acknowledged for making a significant gift. The college then sold the stock in the trust and invested it to produce income for my client. He began receiving a very attractive income from the charitable trust and, in the future when he dies, the college will receive the principal.

By making the gift, his income was significantly greater than if he sold this stock and invested it in an income producing investment. In addition, he removed the stock and its growth from his estate for tax purposes. My client chose the type of charitable remainder trust known as a CRAT. He will receive a set amount of income each month for the rest of his life. This income must be a least 5% of the principal.

If your family is concerned that you are giving away assets that they might inherit, you may choose to use a "Wealth Replacement Trust." With a portion of the amount you get from the charitable remainder trust each year, you pay for a premium on a life insurance policy that replaces the amount given. At your death, the life insurance proceeds are paid into a Wealth Replacement Trust. The proceeds are then paid out to the beneficiaries of the trust based on your wishes.

In some cases, you may want to make a gift to your favorite institutions over a period of time. But you might want to get the tax deduction for the gift this year. Through a very simple vehicle known as a "Donor Advised Fund," you can give a significant amount to a special fund and dole out gifts from it each year to qualified charities as you see fit. When you make the initial gift, you get the tax deduction, and each year you are required to transfer at least 5% of the fund to IRS-approved charities. Many mutual fund companies offer these funds at a very reasonable cost. For approximately 1% per year, they will send out all the checks to the organizations you name and keep a record of each for you. The funds can be invested in a number of different ways, including various types of stocks and bonds.

An extension of the Donor Advised Fund is a "Private Foundation." It acts like a Donor Advised Fund but is much larger in scope. Donors who establish a Private Foundation expect to transfer a very large amount of money to it. Bill Gates is probably the best-known individual who has established a private foundation. He and his wife Melinda gave over 3 billion dollars to establish the "Bill and Melinda Gates Foundation." Their goal has been to improve healthcare throughout the world through their foundation.

It is important to understand that your charitable gifts can be a wonderful way of creating a legacy for yourself that helps an organization that is very meaningful to you. But it is also very important to remember that your wealth is more than just the tangible assets that you pass on to your family and others. Your wealth includes your life story, the values you pass on, the lessons you have learned that you share with others and the impact your stay on this earth will have on future generations.

Remember what Susan Turnbull said in *The Wealth of Your Life*, "What you have learned is as valuable as what you have earned."

7

THE MONEY CONVERSATION

How did you develop your beliefs about money? Was it based on a course you took in school? Or lessons you learned from your parents? Or was it just from observing how your parents acted when dealing with money?

Unfortunately, most of us never had any courses in high school or college relating to personal finance. In shop, we learned how to make a simple bookshelf. In home economics, we learned how to bake a cake. But no one in school ever taught us how to balance a checkbook.

I find this to be one of the greatest shortcomings of American education; ignoring the basics of how to relate to money in our lives.

What is your first memory about money? Mine was bringing a jar full of change to the YMCA every Saturday morning when I was eleven years old. This was where we met with the newspaper delivery staff, who received all the payments I had collected that week on my paper route. My father often helped me with this task, completing the route when I was sick or had just slept late.

The amount I made each week (probably a few dollars) made me feel independent and rich! And from that point on I had a job every summer all the way through college. I had connected having money with independence, and it affected the rest of my life. Other than my time in the Navy, I never had a boss, and I was completely responsible for how much money I made each year.

What is your relationship with money? Do you completely ignore it and let your spouse handle it? Or are you a saver, keeping track of every penny you are able to add to your savings account? Are you a risk taker, making big bets on the next big thing, or a risk avoider, not even sure if you can trust the banks to protect your money? Do you associate spending money and buying things with pleasure or pain?

Why do I ask you these questions? Because whether you know it or not, your relationship and attitude about money has influenced your children and how they relate to money. It is important to begin to understand this connection when you start talking to them about their finances and your own.

As she has done many times in the past, my daughter taught me an important lesson five years ago. She asked me, "Dad, you're a financial planner, and every day you are talking to your clients about money. How come you have never talked to me about it?" I was speechless. I realized that I had never shared our financial goals with her and had never inquired about her own financial situation.

From that day forward we have had an annual financial planning meeting around the Christmas holiday. I share with her what our financial goals are and I ask her what her plans are for the next three to five years. It is a way for each of us to keep our intentions clear and it has been a wonderful tool in cementing our relationship.

At first I had difficulty sharing with her what our income was and how much we had saved for retirement, but after a while, it became much easier. After all, I really didn't have anything to hide. In the same way I had to be careful not to judge her for the amount of credit card debt she had or the amount she had saved.

As each year has progressed, we have become more confident in sharing financial information with each other. She has become more willing to ask me questions about her future and get my input on the best course of action for her to take. And to my constant amazement, her financial situation has improved significantly each year. At this point her income is much higher and she has saved much more than I had at her age. A true miracle!

I believe it is very valuable to have this money conversation with each of your children every year. I suggest strongly that you set a specific date to have a financial meeting with them. Your daughter might expect the meeting on the first day of summer, your son on Father's Day. In this way they will know and look forward to this event.

The first few times may seem uncomfortable, but eventually you will find that you feel much closer and are more honest with each other. You may even find that you have a clearer picture of your own financial goals.

I suggest that you cover the following topics in your annual financial meeting. First share your own financial situation: what your current income is and how much you have saved for retirement. Share with them your goals for retirement. Where do you intend to live? What will your retirement look like? If you are already retired, share what your retirement income is and what you see as your goals for your retirement.

Ask them to share with you their current income and expenses. How much have they saved? Do they have a retirement plan and are they contributing to it? What are their financial goals for three years from now, five years and ten years?

Each year this meeting will become easier. Your children will become confident that you have a handle on your own finances and you will have a clearer picture of what they expect from their future.

Once your children are married, if you have a financial advisor, ask him or her to have an annual meeting with your children and their spouses. After all, if your financial advisor has been successful in helping you accumulate wealth, they will certainly want to build a relationship with the children who will inherit it.

Even though you have connected your children with your financial advisor, it is still valuable to have a financial day with them each year. It's helpful to get their impression of the meeting with their advisor and to share your own goals. You will each look forward to it.

Now that you have begun a serious conversation with your children, it is time to prepare for a full-blown family meeting. In the next chapter we will begin the discussion of how to prepare for this meeting.

8

THE ALPHA CHILD

Now that you have taken the time to gather your information together and have done some serious thinking about your retirement goals, your legacy and your end of life plans, it is time to prepare for the family meeting. The first step in this preparation is to identify who your Alpha Child is.

The Allianz Life Insurance Company conducted a study they defined as "The American Legacies Study." They gathered information by conducting over 2000 interviews with Baby Boomers and their parents. One of the findings their study revealed was the existence of the "Alpha Child." This is the child who keeps the family connected, who is always the first to make sure that family gatherings occur on a consistent basis, and communicates often with his siblings and parents.

He or she is the child who you are most comfortable discussing money issues with. This child will be critical in bringing together your family to discuss your plans.

Take a look at your relationship with your own siblings. Who is the Alpha Child in your family? It may be you. Examine your relationship with your parents. If the above listed characteristics describe you, then you are most likely the Alpha Child. If you are married, discuss it with your spouse and ask for his or her feedback.

Obviously if you are the only child, you may think that you are the Alpha Child. But in some cases, your spouse may act in this capacity. Your parents may have more confidence talking over issues with him or her than they do with you.

I remember when my wife and I decided to move my mom to an assisted living residence near our home. The staff at her independent living community had reported to us that she was getting lost finding her way down to the dining room for dinner and she was often not taking her medication. Several times my wife had driven three hours from our home to take her to a doctor's appointment.

The final straw came when my wife picked her up after a long drive and took her to the doctor's office. When they arrived, the receptionist reported to her that my mother had called the day before and cancelled the appointment. That night when Mary returned home, she gave me an ultimatum: We've got to move your mom closer to us!

So, as the dutiful son, and the only child, its was my job to convince Mom that this move was in her best interest. I was scared to death. What if my mother didn't want to go? What would we do? The next week I met with her at her apartment. I began the conversation with, "Wouldn't you like to be closer to us, Mom?"

She didn't respond; she looked at me blankly. I added, "I think it would be a really good idea if you moved close to us on the Cape. Then we could see you all the time." Again she looked at me with a puzzled look for what seemed like an eternity. Finally she said "Well, what does Mary think?"

For a moment I was speechless. Why was what Mary thought so important? I was her only son, her financial advisor and, I thought, her Alpha Child. Why wasn't she listening to me? But I realized then that in reality my wife was her Alpha Child. From that day forward Mary continued to serve my mom in that role. Whenever there was an important decision to be made, my mother looked to Mary for advice.

It is important for you to identify who is your Alpha Child. Who is the child your other children respect? Which child do you ask for feedback? Which child acts as a leader in the family?

Once you have identified who the Alpha Child is, it's important to have a conversation with him or her, preferably face to face. Share with her that you would like to have a meeting with the whole family. Make it clear that you feel it is important for you to share with them the plans and preparations you have made for your retirement years. Tell them that it is essential to discuss things now, while everyone is healthy and can make important decisions.

Your child's first response might be, as my daughter's was, "We don't need to talk about that now, Dad. You are healthy. You are doing fine." But don't back off. Yes, this is a difficult discussion, and it might be easy just to put it off but don't. Respond with, "And that's exactly why we want to meet now. Mom and I have discussed this and it is really important to us to get together. OK?"

Hopefully your child will recognize your sincerity and go along with your decision. But if not, take a step back and acknowledge her difficulty in dealing with her parents' mortality. In any case leave her with a copy of your completed "Five Wishes" and your spouse's as well. Add, "I'd like you to take a look at these.

Mom and I have spent a lot of time preparing them and we'd like to get your feedback. We don't have to discuss it now, but I'd like to arrange a time when we can review them together."

Agree on a follow-up date to review your "Five Wishes" and discuss the family meeting in more detail. Before you have the follow-up meeting with your child, make sure they have read the documents. In many cases they may want to put it off and not even think about your demise. But insist that they read the documents and set a date to get back together.

At the follow-up meeting you may want to spend some time discussing the Five Wishes. Your child may have some questions or comments. Or she might respond that she has read it and understood your wishes. That's fine too. What is most important is that you have opened up the conversation.

Then it is time to move on to a discussion about the family meeting. First it is important to stress that this is not just a family social gathering, but a time to talk seriously about important issues. I recommend that you insist that spouses and children not attend this meeting. Small children would certainly be a distraction and adding significant others might change the whole dynamic of the meeting. But this is your decision. There might be circumstances where adding a spouse is critical. But only if that child is disabled or unable to make any decisions without the spouse's consent.

Ask your Alpha child if she would be willing to communicate your meeting plans to her siblings, or if she would rather you do it. I think the invitation to the meeting would likely have more weight if it came from your child. Her siblings would tell her how they really feel about the idea. Stress to her that her participation is vital in making the meeting a success.

Ask her to get back to you with the responses of her siblings. They may tell her that they are too busy or that they are not really interested in participating in this meeting. They may say that they don't get along with a certain brother or sister and don't want to attend. But the Alpha Child must insist that this meeting is critical and everyone must be there. I have participated in meetings where siblings who did not get along were able to come together to help their parents. I have participated in family meetings where the children gathered together from locations thousands of miles away. But their willingness to meet proved to be a life changing event for the whole family.

The Family Meeting may be the first time that all the siblings have gotten together with their parents to talk about something really important. They may not realize that initially, but when they get together they will understand how important their gathering is. You must impress upon your Alpha Child that this will happen.

If by any chance, one of your children is out of the country or for some reason just cannot make it back to a meeting at your home, insist that they participate in some way, either through Skype, or Facetime, or even a conference call. If any child is left out, it is possible that they may use this to discredit the decisions that were made at the meeting. "Well I wasn't there. And I don't think that's a good idea." It is important that each child be involved in the decision making process or at least be present when it occurs. Without this context they may not understand why certain plans were made. They might dispute decisions without understanding the rationale behind them.

Once you have recruited your Alpha Child to participate, it is time to move on to the next steps to prepare the family meeting. In the next chapter we will discuss the steps you need to take.

9

PREPARING FOR
THE FAMILY MEETING

Now that you have met with your Alpha Child, shared your Five Wishes document with him/her and discussed your desire to have a family meeting, it is time to plan the meeting itself. You may have gotten some initial resistance from your Alpha Child about their role in organizing the meeting, but you made it clear to them how important this meeting is to you. Sharing and discussing the critical issues you will face as you get older is essential in assuring that your family will work together to make decisions. The family meeting can lead to a breakthrough in communication and family relationships if structured properly.

Carefully planning out the meeting will assure its success. If you have met with your Alpha Child, you have completed one of the most important steps. The second step is to decide upon a facilitator. You can certainly run the meeting yourself, but I suggest strongly that you consider having someone else do it. As a member of the family, you are automatically emotionally involved in the process. As much as you may wish to remain objective and neutral, certain topics will affect your judgment. Selecting an independent party who can remain calm and cool will take the burden of managing the process off of your shoulders.

How Do You Select the Facilitator?

Who should you select as the facilitator? If you have a financial advisor, he or she might be a good candidate. This person has probably gotten to know your financial situation very well over time, has earned your trust, and has proven that they can work with you. Bringing them in as the facilitator might serve another purpose as well. It is an opportunity for them to get to know your children and your spouse (if they haven't already). Eventually your financial advisor may have to work with your family to transfer your assets. It would be very helpful if your advisor was acquainted with your children and had the opportunity to earn their trust and facilitate the process.

If you don't feel that your financial advisor is the right choice, you might select your family attorney, your religious leader or another professional advisor to fill the role. You might even consider a friend who is active in business or the community. In addition, you may have a local organization that provides facilitation services. On Cape Cod, where I live, a non-profit organization known as Cape Mediation has several trained facilitators available who are experienced in working with families in all types of situations. Do a Google search on "facilitation" or "mediation services" and add your location to find out if such a group exists in your area.

What makes a good facilitator?

A good facilitator is a person who is a good listener. In addition, that person should be well-organized and empathetic. The individual must have the skill to elicit responses from family members, but know when to cut them short if they are straying off topic or pursuing their own agenda. It is important that family members respect the facilitator but not feel that he or she is aloof. The facilitator must understand that he or she is not involved in the meeting to provide therapy or heal the family's emotional issues. Her role is to facilitate discussion on the topics selected and help the family develop a plan of action.

The Intake Process

The facilitator's first job is to meet with the Alpha Child and get the contact information for other family members. He then needs to contact each of the family members for a one-on-one conversation. It's fine to have this conversation over the phone.

In this introductory conversation, the facilitator will explain the process and philosophy of the family meeting to each family member. He will explain that the parents requested that all children attend the meeting. He will explain that the meeting is set up to share ideas and concerns and to develop a plan to help the parents make decisions for their later years. He will point out that the meeting is to be non-confrontational and will be conducted in an environment of mutual respect. (I will share more details of the meeting in the next chapter.)

During the conversation the facilitator will want to learn:

1. What the family member's interest is in having a meeting.

2. What the family member's concerns are about having a meeting.

3. What the participant thinks the concerns of other family members might be.

4. What topics the family member considers most important to discuss at the meeting.

5. What topics the family member believes should be included in the meeting (this can be done anonymously).

The facilitator must make it clear to the family member that their conversation is confidential and will not be shared with anyone else, unless the family member requests it be shared. Each person must feel free to speak candidly without fear that there will be repercussions for whatever he or she might say.

The facilitator should ask each participant to prepare comments to share at the start of the family meeting—their concerns, their wishes, their goals for the meeting. In addition, each person should write down something positive about each family member that they might be asked to share. This focus will start off the meeting in a positive direction and avoid the possibility of it becoming a gripe session.

The purpose of this Intake Conversation is threefold:

1. The facilitator wants to make sure each participant understands the process and purpose of the meeting.

2. The facilitator wants to find out what is most important to the participant and what their major concerns are.

3. The facilitator wants to make the participant confortable, address any objections they may have to the meeting and create a bond with them.

Creating an Agenda

Once the facilitator has conducted the intake phone calls, he should have enough information to create a preliminary agenda. The agenda should include the topics that the parents want to include in the meeting. It should also address any additional topics that the adult children request.

The facilitator should then circulate the proposed agenda to everyone in the family and request feedback. He should make sure that everyone has received the preliminary agenda and has had the opportunity to respond. If the agenda is sent out via email, he needs to get a confirmation from everyone that they received it. Based on the feedback he receives, he can then prepare a final agenda.

The facilitator needs to coordinate the time and place of the meeting with the parents and the Alpha Child. It is the Alpha Child's job to then communicate this date to her siblings to make sure that the date works for everyone. This is often difficult due to the complexity of everyone's schedule. It may be necessary to schedule a date three to four months out to make sure everyone can attend. In most cases it makes sense to have the meeting at the parents' home. If there is not space to accommodate all the family members, another neutral location should be selected.

Once the time and place of the meeting have been agreed upon, the facilitator should send out the final agenda with that information. In the period between this communication and the meeting itself, the facilitator may get some comments or messages from family members regarding their concerns, interests or opinions. Throughout this process the facilitator needs to reinforce with them the importance of the meeting. He may have to neutralize any fears or considerations that family members may have. The objective is to make sure that the meeting actually occurs.

In the next chapter we will discuss the conduct of the meeting itself.

10

THE FAMILY MEETING

The family meeting can be a life-changing experience for the entire family if it is conducted properly. Most families have never before gathered together as a group to discuss critical family issues. This family meeting will probably be the first time they sit down together with a specific agenda and an outside facilitator who will direct their conversation.

It is important that everyone in the family enters into this discussion with a certain level of trust and compassion. Family members are more likely to share their feelings honestly if they know they will not be verbally attacked or criticized. The purpose of the meeting is to clarify and discuss your plans for the future and the role each family member will play in your life as you face the aging process.

The family meeting is not the setting to bring up old conflicts between various members of the family, such as who Mom or Dad favor more, who has gotten financial help and who has not been in communication with their siblings. The focus should be on helping you discuss your options, sharing your plans and developing a realistic course of action.

The facilitator will open up the meeting by stating some basic ground rules. This includes the predicted length of the meeting, whether or not follow-up sessions are planned and the times of scheduled breaks. He will select a family member to act as scribe, documenting topics that were discussed, decisions that were made and follow up that needs to happen. He will then discuss the Consensus Building Model, which will be used to formulate decisions during the family meeting.

The Consensus Building Model

The Consensus Building Model is a way for a family to reach a nearly unanimous agreement and then implement that agreement successfully. It avoids the traditional method of taking a vote on important matters, which inevitably creates a discontented minority. No one person can dominate the conversation to get their selection implemented.

The facilitator will help the family define those points in which a decision has to be made. Rather than take a vote to determine what specific course of action should be taken, the facilitator will ask each person to respond with one of six assessments.

A. "I wholeheartedly agree."

B. "It is a good idea."

C. "I can live with it."

D. "I have reservations. I want to talk."

E. "I have serious reservations. I must talk."

F. "I cannot be a part of this decision. I must block it."

For a consensus to occur, all members of the family must reach A, B or C. Anyone who designates D, E or F must clearly explain their concerns and provide a "constructive alternative." Everyone's voice must be heard. Decisions are reached through compromise and understanding. If a consensus cannot be reached after extensive discussion, the facilitator can choose to table the topic and return to it later when participants have had more time to think about it.

The Circle Process

Once the facilitator has laid out the ground rules, he will ask each participant to make a statement regarding his/her goals for the meeting. What does he or she hope the results of the meeting will be? It is not an opportunity for each person to complain about what is not working, but an opportunity to express their hopes for what will work. Each person must be given an opportunity to speak without interruption. If there are a number of interruptions, the facilitator may choose to implement the Circle Process.

The Circle Process has been used successfully in schools to create positive classroom climates and resolve behavior problems, in the workplace to deal with conflicts, in prisons to reduce violent behavior and in social services to develop support systems for people struggling to make sense of their lives.

It is a simple process based on the ancient Native American tradition of gathering around a fire and passing the talking piece from person to person. In the family setting, members position themselves to be able to see each of the other family members. They can be sitting in a circle of chairs in the living room or around a circular table. The facilitator selects a talking piece (a small article of significance to the family) that can be passed around from person to person.

The holder of the talking piece has an opportunity to talk while all other participants listen. He or she may choose to offer silence and pass the piece without talking. There is no obligation to speak when the talking piece comes. (*The Little Book of Circle Processes,* Kay Pranis)

The talking piece is a critical element of the Circle Process. It assures the speaker that he will not be interrupted and will be able to pause and reflect on what he wants to say. It creates a level of order that allows the expression of difficult emotions without the process spinning out of control. It is a powerful equalizer, allowing each participant to speak, while carrying the implicit understanding that each person has something valuable to say.

Once the initial comments are made, the facilitator will then guide the family through the agreed-upon agenda. The facilitator will maintain a neutral position, not expressing opinions on the validity of anyone's comments, but acknowledging them when they have spoken. The facilitator is not an enforcer, but a monitor.

Listening

It is important for each participant in the family meeting to make the effort to become a good listener. People rarely feel really listened to. "When another person is totally with you, leaning in, interested in every word, eager to empathize, you feel known and understood." (*Co-Active Coaching*, Whitworth)

Most people do not listen at a very deep level. It seems that our attention spans are getting shorter and shorter as we are distracted by text messages, emails and the internet. According to Whitworth, Kimsey-House and Sandahl (*Co-Active Coaching*), there are three levels to listening.

Most of the time we stay at the first level of listening. We listen to the words of the other person, but we are concentrating on what these words mean to us. The focus is on what you said and what I said. The spotlight is on me, my thoughts, my feelings, my conclusions about myself.

There are many times when level one listening is appropriate. When you are traveling or when you are in a restaurant, it makes a great deal of sense to stay at level one. You just want to gather relevant information that is useful to you.

In level two listening you are intently focused on the other person. You can tell when people are communicating at this level. They are leaning toward each other, paying specific attention to each other and not paying attention to the outside world around them.

In level two you listen for the other person's words, their expression and their emotions. You notice many details of their communication, if they are happy or sad, if they are energized or depressed. Level two listening happens most often when you are coaching another person or expressing your feelings in a one-on-one relationship. It can be very satisfying in a conversation with one of your children or your spouse.

Level three listening is often called global listening. You listen as though you were at the center of life, receiving information from everything and everyone around you. Very rarely does anyone operate at level three. It involves all the senses. What you see, what you hear, smell and feel are all important. At this level you have much greater access to your intuition. You receive information that is not directly observable.

To listen at level three you must be open and sensitive to everything around you, ready to receive information from all your senses. It happens rarely, but when you have reached that level, you will know it.

Take note of the level of listening you are engaged in at the family meeting. Are you listening to your son but focusing more on what his words mean to you? Or are you listening to him with the attention on his feelings and his concerns? Notice the conversation in your head. Is it more about you or more about him? The more you can stay at level two, the more impact the meeting will have on you.

At some point you may find yourself at level three. At this level you will begin to notice the overall experience of your family. You may feel as if you are an observer looking down on this meeting as if from another planet. It will give you an interesting insight on how to handle the issues your family is dealing with. You can't get to level three with more effort. It will come naturally or not at all.

The Meeting Agenda

Based on the conversations the facilitator had with each of the participants ahead of time, a number of different items may be on the agenda for the family meeting. But certain items should be covered in all family meetings. They are the following:

Leaving a Legacy

It is important that you make it clear to your children what you want your legacy to be. What are the values and beliefs that you want to be remembered for? What are the life lessons that you want to share with them? Are there specific organizations or groups that you want to leave a significant gift to? As we discussed in Chapter 6, it would be very valuable if you created a Legacy Letter to share with them at the meeting.

Legal Issues

There are certain legal documents that your family must understand. It is not a good idea to share your will with them during the meeting, but it is important for them to know that you have one and what its purpose is. They also need to know who the executor of the will is, or the person that will carry out the directions that you specified in the will. It may be your spouse, one of your children, a friend or advisor. But they should know who that person is and what their job will be.

Now is also a good time to share with them whom you have designated to hold your durable power of attorney. This is the person who will make financial decisions for each of you if you cannot. In addition to your spouse, another person should also have that power if for some reason your spouse is not available or is not competent. It may be one of your children or someone outside the family. You should identify who has the power for each of you and what their responsibility will be.

You should also explain who your health care proxy is and what their responsibility is. If you have completed "The Five Wishes," now would be a good time to give each of your children a copy and ask them to read it. (I have described it in more detail in Chapter 5.) Let your family know that you will answer any questions they have after they have read it. They may want to know the details of how you want to be cared for if you are seriously ill and under what circumstances you don't want to be kept alive. This can be a very sensitive but important discussion.

Health Care

There are three basic health care questions you must answer for your children in the family meeting. First, if you or your spouse need long term care, where will you live? Can you continue to live in your home? Is the home accessible if one of you needs a wheelchair? If you can't stay in the home, where will you live? Will you buy a condo or become part of a retirement community? Share your thoughts with them. Get their feedback. You may not have made any decisions yet, but their feedback may help you make that decision.

Secondly, if one of you needs continuing care, who will provide it? Will one spouse take care of the other? Or do you expect a daughter or daughter-in-law to be the caregiver? Are you going to seek outside help? It's important for the family to know this now and not be suddenly surprised with your expectations when one of you has a health care crisis.

Finally, if one of you needs long term care, how do you expect to pay for that care? If you have long term care insurance, explain to your children how this insurance works. If you don't have this insurance, it's important for your family to understand that you will pay for care out of your personal resources. Read over Chapter 5 for more details on funding the cost of long term care.

Finances

The fourth important area that must be discussed at the family meeting is the area of finances. Many people freak out when they think that they might have to reveal their financial situation to their children. I remember when I was preparing for a family meeting a few years ago. I had a conversation with the Alpha child and he informed me, "Dad is willing to go through with this meeting, but he does not want to talk about his finances. Don't even bring it up!"

We started the family meeting on a Friday night at the parents' lovely home. The four adult children were there with them (two had flown in from across the country). The evening session went extremely well and everyone was surprised at how much they had accomplished in one session. Within three hours the room had made a dramatic shift from nervousness to closeness and intimacy.

The following morning I returned to the home for a Saturday session. It was scheduled to begin at 9:00 am. I arrived at 8:30 and noticed that Dad was placing a piece of paper on everyone's chair. I was surprised and asked him what the paper was. He responded "It's my financial statement. I decided that if I'm going to do this thing right, I need to be in it 100%!"

I was amazed. Within twenty-four hours he had shifted from being a resistant skeptic to being open and eager to contribute. But don't worry. You don't have to reveal your entire balance sheet to your children as he did. All your children really want to know is if you are financially secure and won't need their financial help. Of course if you think you might need their support, you need to make them aware of this at the meeting.

There is another item that needs to be discussed in more detail. It's the family real estate. What will become of your property when you and your spouse are deceased? Don't just leave it up to the children to figure it out after you are gone. I have seen a loving family turn into a very angry crowd when they can't agree on the disposition of family property. It is important to discuss with the children what you would like to happen to it. Does one of them want to buy it? Do they all want to share in the costs if it is an attractive vacation property? Now is the time to find that out and work out a plan for the disposition of the property so it doesn't become a source of contention later on.

One final issue that needs to be discussed is **"What will happen to all our stuff when we are gone?"** I can remember having a family meeting with an older couple and their four adult children and noticed that Mom was getting very anxious. At first I thought her anxiety was due to the fact that she was preparing to discuss her end of life planning with her children.

But when I asked her what her concern was, she responded, "I don't know what I am going to do with all my stuff! I have several beautiful collections and I don't want my children fighting over the objects right after my funeral or just putting them out in the yard for a giant tag sale!"

She admitted to me that she hadn't slept for several nights thinking about this terrible possibility. She confided in me that her husband still wasn't talking to his sister after 20 years because she had raided the house when their parents died and taken everything of value before he had even arrived. "I don't want that happening in my family!" she proclaimed.

So what did we do? I asked her to describe her valuable collections to her children at the family meeting. She then created a list of all the items and asked each child to review them. If they wanted an item, they were asked to put their name next to it. If more than one wanted something, they both listed their names next to it and mom would decide who got it.

Mom collected the lists after the family meeting, reviewed them over the next few weeks and then reported to her children who would get what. No one disputed her decisions. After all, the collections were hers and she could give them to charity if she chose. The next time I talked to her I noticed her anxiety level was significantly lower. She told me that for the first time in a long time she was sleeping very soundly.

If you are a parent, don't do your children a disservice. Don't leave it up to them to decide what to do with your stuff after you are gone. The loveliest relationships are often spoiled by siblings fighting over the silver forks. Decide to use the method I have just discussed or tell them what you intend to do with your stuff. It may create some initial upset, but in the long run it will save much grief and anxiety for the whole family.

Concluding the Meeting

It is very important to conclude the meeting in a positive way. The facilitator should ask the child who was designated as the scribe to summarize decisions that were made and the follow-up steps that were agreed upon. If it is not clear who will be doing the follow up and when, now is the time to clarify. Everyone needs to feel accountable for the results of the meeting. The facilitator should request volunteers to complete the follow-up tasks if no one was designated.

The facilitator should ask each participant what the meeting has meant to them. I have been very moved by the words that were shared by family members at the end of these meetings. Many times I have observed that relationships within the family have been transformed by these conversations.

One of the emails I received from a family member sums up the results I have observed from family meetings:

"This meeting was productive, respectful, creative and unifying. We experienced evidence that we can converse and decide matters in a way that keeps the family connected rather than drifting apart due to unresolved issues or disagreement. I didn't expect perfect harmony and total agreement on all matters, just a healthy respect of everyone's opinions. We walked away identifying the important decisions we have to make, who should make them and when they need to be decided upon. And that made the meeting a great success."

I have been the facilitator for a number of families who held family meetings. In almost every case I noted a dramatic shift in how family members treated each other after the meeting. For many of them it was the first time they had a serious conversation about important issues that would be facing the whole family. And after the meeting they had a much better understanding of how they could work together and trust each other.

11

SPECIAL SITUATIONS

It is relatively simple to communicate your wishes to your family if you only have one spouse and children with only that spouse. But what if you are remarried and have a second family? Communication with everyone becomes much more complicated.

Second Marriages

One of my clients, a recently retired doctor, was in his seventies when he discovered that his wife had cancer. She became increasingly sick and incapacitated. Fortunately, one of her best friends, a widow, came and lived with them and took care of my client's dying wife in her last days. During her months of care giving, the friend became very close to the doctor. Within a year after his wife's passing, he married her best friend and caretaker.

Early on in the marriage, the new wife confided in me that her greatest fear was that if her new husband died, his children would demand that the home was theirs and force her to leave. I wasn't really surprised when about a year after their marriage, the doctor called me and told me that they were going to sell their current home and build a new one. It was clear that his new wife had taken control to protect her interests. The new home was based on her design and ideas, and the doctor spent a great deal of his wealth having it built and decorated.

My client could have protected his new wife if he had redrafted his will and named her to inherit the home. If he had done this, his wife would get the house when he died, and then when she died, the house would go to her children. A better option for his children would be to give his new wife the life use of the property and then pass it on to to his children at her death. His children would still eventually get the property, but they would have to wait until she passed away. But his new wife pressed him to build a new home for her and he agreed. Unfortunately I never had the opportunity to discuss these options with him.

In another situation, a client of mine retired after a long career as a very well-known family physician. Shortly after he retired, he learned that his wife had Alzheimer's. The first few years of his retirement were occupied with taking care of her and finally putting her into a nursing home. Within months, she no longer knew who he was. He was very lonely and depressed and contacted the widow of another doctor who had been a long-time friend. They started seeing each other often, and their meetings turned into a romantic relationship. Shortly after his first wife died, he married the widow of his close friend.

Although his new wife lived a very luxurious lifestyle and had a very strong balance sheet, she didn't have a great deal of cash, or at least she didn't want to spend it. I noticed my client taking increasingly larger withdrawals from his retirement plan. After several months of watching this pattern, I called him in to discuss the situation. He informed me that he was loaning the money to his new wife to completely renovate her very large old house and to purchase a condo in Florida. Unfortunately, every withdrawal he took from his IRA to help her pay expenses was taxable as income to him.

Since the time of his remarriage, I have watched his retirement plan get smaller and smaller. Recently, I made it clear to him that he probably would run out of money within the next two years. At age 76, he will have to depend entirely on his new wife for income the rest of his life. He seemed powerless to do anything about the situation. I informed him that the worst possible situation might be if his wife predeceased him and her children expected their inheritance. He would be left destitute.

Protecting Your Family in Second Marriages

Unfortunately, in neither of these situations were the children of my clients aware of what was happening to their father's assets. Unless I observed some inability of the client to act or think rationally, I had no right to inform the adult children. These individuals were my clients and I was required to keep their financial affairs confidential. But what could children do if they saw their parent entering into a situation with a new wife or husband who was quickly going through their assets?

The first step would be for the children to have a meeting with their parent to discuss the situation. This is often very difficult because it puts the children in a position of appearing to be money-hungry heirs, even if they are acting in their parent's best interest. Most likely their parent will defend his actions as merely trying to take care of his spouse. In the end, he has the right to spend his money any way he wants without answering to his children.

If the children believed their parent was no longer acting rationally and was making decisions that were random and irresponsible, they could request that their parent be declared incompetent, and have one of them named as his conservator. This would give them the authority to manage his financial affairs. This is a difficult and time-consuming process. Generally, the parent's attending physician must certify the individual's incompetency. A hearing is set in probate court and conducted by a probate judge. The attending physician will have to testify that the parent is not capable of making financial decisions. An attorney can represent the parent.

If the judge rules that the parent is incompetent, he or she will name a conservator. The conservator must be of good character and capable of effectively managing the parent's affairs. The judge could name a healthy spouse or one of the parent's adult children as conservator. Once the adult child or spouse is named conservator, he or she must file an annual accounting with the probate court. This accounting lists every transaction that the conservator conducted with the parent's money. In most cases, the conservator hires an accountant and a lawyer to complete this report.

The way to avoid this uncomfortable situation in the first place is for you to do some planning in advance. It would be best for you to meet with the attorney who drafted your wills and trusts and discuss what happens to your assets when one of you dies and the surviving spouse remarries. This may be a very difficult conversation, but it is valuable to have while you are both healthy and thinking clearly. Often an attorney will suggest having a certain portion of your assets go into a trust. A separate trustee is named (other than your surviving spouse) who oversees the assets. Your surviving spouse has access to the income from the trust and limited access to the principal. At the death of your surviving spouse, the assets then go to the children or grandchildren.

By setting up this trust, you avoid the possibility of a second spouse diverting all of your assets to their children from a previous marriage.

Special Needs Children

You may have a child who has had a serious accident and suffered permanent injury, suffers from serious mental illness or was born with a mental or physical disability. You may be concerned that when you die there will be no one left to care for your child or no one who has the assets to make sure that they are taken care of properly. You should consult with an estate planning attorney to set up a special needs trust. It is sometimes called a "Supplemental Needs Trust." This is a very unique trust designed to protect an individual who has a disability.

A Special Needs or Supplemental Needs Trust enables a person with a physical or mental disability or a chronic illness to have held in trust for his or her benefit an unlimited amount of assets. If the trust is drafted properly, these assets are not counted for disqualification from Medicaid. In other words, the individual can still qualify for Medicaid payments or social security disability payments and have a significant amount of assets within this trust. Normally, a person must be impoverished to qualify for Medicaid; however, it is usually the case that these assets revert to the government to reimburse them for Medicaid payments if the individual should die.

One of my clients has an adult child who had a motorcycle accident and suffered a serious brain injury. The son now lives at home with his parents, who are retired. They have two other children; however, one of these children is a daughter who is a single mother with two young children. The other is a son who has settled about 3000 miles away with his own family. As a result, my clients don't believe that either of these children could be expected to take care of their brother. They have set up a Special Needs Trust for that child, which will be funded primarily with life insurance. My clients purchased a special type of life insurance known as a second-to-die policy. When the second spouse dies, the life insurance proceeds will be paid into the trust. These funds will then be used for the care of the disabled child.

Irresponsible Children (Or Children's Spouses)

There are other situations where you may want to protect your assets when children are irresponsible or have an irresponsible spouse. One of your children might have a spouse who is a notorious big spender and completely irresponsible with money, or one of your children might have a serious drug, gambling or alcohol problem. In each of these situations, you might be reluctant to leave your child with a large amount of money, which they might spend irresponsibly.

In their book *Beyond the Grave*, Gerald and Jeffrey Condon describe an excellent way to protect the inheritance of one of your children that might have an addiction, a credit problem, marital problems or other financial difficulties. It is called a "Protection Trust." When you die, your money and property does not go directly to the difficult child. It goes to the trustee of the Protection Trust. The trustee manages all the assets that go into this trust, which may include real estate, stocks, bonds, cash, and even jewelry.

The trustee also makes decisions regarding the distribution of income or any principal to the child. He makes these decisions based on the instructions made by you in the trust before you died. The amount of protection built into the trust is based on your desire to control the spending of your money by that child after you are gone. One of your child's brothers or sisters could be named the trustee, but it might be better to name a trusted advisor or possibly an institution as trustee. It could be very difficult for another family member to act as trustee, especially if the child puts a lot of pressure on them to have access to the money. A third option would be to have an institution be co-trustees with one of your children or your trusted advisor.

One of my clients had named his daughter to be one of the trustees of his estate. When she was younger, she had difficulties managing an alcohol problem, but had gotten married, had children and seemed to be getting her life on track. One day my client called me, clearly distressed, and told me that his daughter had disappeared. One night when her husband came home, she had said she had to go out and pick something up at the store. She didn't return from the store and was missing for several weeks. They later learned she had gone on an alcohol binge. My client asked that she be removed as a trustee of his assets and that a protection trust be set up for her. The trust would provide an income for her, but stipulated that if she had another relapse or could not control herself, the money would be cut off.

Dealing with all the family issues that may arise can be very challenging. You will never have all the answers you need to do everything perfectly when you pass on your assets to your children. All you can do is try to make the right decisions for your family and inform them of what you are doing and why.

You may choose to ignore family difficulties and hope that things will just work out. But if you do, you are setting your family up for misunderstanding, miscommunication and disaster. The Family Meeting is the perfect place to share with your children your plans and why you have made them.

12

WHAT'S NEXT?

If you have followed my recommendations, gotten your financial house in order and then communicated your wishes to your children, you should be feeling pretty good about yourself. You have done more than 90% of your contemporaries would ever consider. You should feel comfortable knowing that you and your family have prepared for whatever circumstances you might face.

You might think that you can relax now that you have accomplished so much. But I would suggest that this is just the beginning. You have established a new level of communication with your family and created an opening for all kinds of wonderful things to happen.

I recommend that you take the following six steps now that the basic work is done.

1. Review the notes that your scribe recorded during the family meeting. Determine what areas still require follow-up.

2. Assign various family members to do the follow-up on the outstanding issues and give them a deadline to report back to you.

3. Six months after the family meeting, prepare a review that indicates which follow-up issues have been completed and which are still outstanding. Share this review with your family.

4. Consider making the family meeting an annual event. Subsequent annual meetings do not have to be as long as the initial meeting; they can simply include updates on progress in certain areas.

5. Plan and hold an annual financial meeting with your spouse. Review with him/her the goals that the two of you have established for your retirement years and what progress you have made on them. Select a specific date to do this every year, like New Year's Day or the Saturday before the Super Bowl.

6. Set up annual financial planning meetings with each of your children. Ask them to prepare a balance sheet prior to this meeting that shows their assets and any debts they have. Also ask them to share with you their financial goals for the next five, ten and twenty years. This may be hard for them to do, especially if they have never made financial goals before. And they may choose not to share their finances with you now that they are adults. But it is worth asking them to have an annual meeting.

Creating a financial planning meeting with each of your children can be a very satisfying experience. First of all, it requires them to annually take stock of where they are—an exercise that the majority of their friends are not doing. Secondly, it gives you an opportunity to have an in-depth discussion with them about their future. It will strengthen your relationship with them if you view this activity in a positive light.

Do not use this meeting to scold your children for what they are not doing or what they are doing wrong. That will quickly shut down the meeting and discourage them from ever agreeing to future ones. Look for opportunities to praise them. Give them constructive, useful criticism. This is another opportunity for you to become a good listener and not a lecturer.

Final Thoughts

Writing this book has been a very satisfying experience for me. I have updated my own plans as I worked through the chapters. It became very clear to me that intergenerational planning is a dynamic process. As your family circumstances change, your plans must change too.

Don't leave this book on the back shelf. Keep it nearby, where you can refer back to it periodically. And don't forget that the most important message of this book is a very simple one. Communication and relationship are the tools that make a family work. Always remember that the greatest gift you can give your spouse and your children is the willingness to share your thoughts, seek feedback and communicate openly.

By following the steps I have outlined in this book, getting your financial house in order and communicating your plans and concerns with your family, you will find that you finally have peace of mind. Once you have taken the steps to organize and share your financial future with your family, you will be confident that you are prepared to face whatever the future holds.

Happiness

Is a function of accepting what is.

Love

Is a function of communication.

Health

Is a function of participation.

Self Expression

Is a function of responsibility.

Werner Erhard, 1973

ABOUT THE AUTHOR

For 33 years Bob Mauterstock was a financial adviser to hundreds of families in Connecticut. Bob became a registered investment adviser in 1982. He achieved the designation of Certified Financial Planner in 1987.

Bob retired at the end of 2009. For the last ten years of his practice he was the CEO of KR Wealth Management in Farmington, Connecticut. Bob specialized in retirement income planning, long term care planning and investment management. He wrote his first book in 2008 entitled, **"Can We Talk? A Financial Guide for Baby Boomers Assisting Their Elderly Parents."**

Since he retired, Bob has been speaking to groups throughout the country about communication between baby boomers and their families regarding the critical issues of aging. In addition he began a program to coach financial advisors to give their clients "the gift of communication" and become the family's trusted advisor for future generations.

Bob lives with his wife, Mary in Cape Cod, Massachusetts. Their daughter, Stephanie, lives in New York City.

If you wish to contact Bob to arrange a speaking engagement or discuss any of the material in this book email him at bob@giftofcommunication.com. You can learn more about his work from his website **www.giftofcommunication.com**.

He also writes about issues of aging in his blog **www.parentcareplanning.wordpress.com**.

79456686R00060

Made in the USA
Middletown, DE
10 July 2018